LITTLE NOTES OF ANGUISH

AND OTHER POEMS

SNEHA JAISWAL

To you

For the sheer rebellious act of reading poetry

Contents

1. Not Dead... 1

2. In The Naivety... 3

3. What Is 'closure'... 4

4. For A Moment... 5

5. Does Disease... 6

6. The Unwelcome Patter... 7

7. There Are Dried Petals... 8

8. The Wind... 10

9. How Are You... 11

10. Why Is Sorry... 13

11. The Floor... 15

12. Why... 16

13. It's Easy... 18

14. I Want To Be... 20

15. We Are Like... 22

16. If I Had... 23

17. Our Anxieties... 24

18. I Don't Seek... 25

19. I Don't Need... 26

20. How Desperate... 28

21. We Don't Always... 29

22. A Song... 30

23. I've Cut Someone... 32

24. The Little Rushbird... 33

Contents

25. To You... 34
26. What Would You... 36
27. Dysmorphia... 37
28. They Said... 38
29. Ants... 39
30. I've Only Felt... 41
31. Myths... 42
32. The Air... 43
33. Some Days... 44
34. Blue... 46
35. Who Knows... 47
36. Show Me... 48
37. They Can... 50
38. Maybe... 51
39. Broken... 52
40. Pull... 53
41. There's A Familiar... 54
42. People... 55
More Titles By Sneha Jaiswal 57
Connect With The Author 59

1. Not dead...

Not dead yet, so I'll speak for myself
Don't be my voice, don't borrow my tale
I can spell my desires, they aren't on sale
I can spot allies and those who deceive
Don't tell me what I can be or must be
I don't want to be 'that girl'
I don't want to be 'that boy'
I want to be the wind
That can pass you by
I want to be the sky
Away from your eye
That can only look down
Or until just the nose
Jutting in unwanted nooks
Passing sentences on looks
I don't want to be 'that man'
I don't want to be 'that woman'
I want to be the mountain
That can withstand all fires
I want to be the ocean
That can drown out vicious noise
Or maybe I could be invisible

Like the air we breathe
Everywhere, indispensable
But free, without any label

2. In the naivety...

In the naivety of youth, travel seemed a worthy goal
World map on the bedroom wall pointing pretty places
But soon, just the warmth of our home was enough
There's joy in fresh meals, comfort in familiar faces
Let the daredevils pack their bags & fly where they want
To fancy suite bookings, or cheap dingy dormitories
I'll be in a cosy corner of my room with some stories
Clacking of keys exploring wherever dreams can land
Now I make plans of weeks I don't want to step out
Marking calendars with visits of dear friends of mine
We will meet at home, eat, talk, laugh and drink wine
Take a walk in the neighbourhood, coo over cats or dogs
Wanderlust ads are in vain now, no matter how bright
A new book a week is bliss, so is the same bed each night
No itineraries to be made, no 'where, when and how'
Once a treasure, who knows where that map is now

3. What is 'closure'...

What is 'closure' but a mirage in the desert
For somethings may never have a neat end
It's just a crutch, a word on the deep end
towards which we cannot hope to swim
'Closure' is a word of denial, of false comfort
For what do you do when someone just dies?
Leaving behind chaos, and a boatful of lies
Do you hold a seance? Or try an ouija board?
Will you keep a list of your questions ready?
For when that moment of 'closure' comes
cue dramatic music, a slow flourish of drums
Expect answers to soothe all your pain
You'll get all possible responses one can find
And the classic suggestion of a "fresh start"
But it won't fill the empty wells of your heart
For 'closure' is but a mirage, a sleight of mind

4. For a moment...

For a moment... let there be void
An emptiness that's not bereaving
But a blanket that's comforting
Like a newborn sleeping in peace
Dreaming of nothing
Wanting of nothing
No riches or notes to thieve
No motives to deceive
The self or those around
Nothingness has its own rewards
No loss, no burden of things to be found
Things not afforded by cash or cards
Let some days be blank frames
Luxurious art-pieces worth infinity
Seconds spent in ruminations not games
Breaking chains only normal, not asininity

5. Does disease...

Does disease delight in death?
In its slow spread & a quick end
Breaking us with every breath
Till there's no more to bend
And no dreams to see
But the black of nothing
That now roams free
In our eyes that sting
The softest sheets fail
No silken touch can dare
Let any respite ever sail
Into the mind's care
Too absorbed in blame
To every second name
Even daughters or sons
Every presence burns
For their sun won't set
Their horizons bright
Sweet summers to be met
While we shiver in fright

6. The unwelcome patter...

The unwelcome patter calls
A chill comes with the drops
Seeping through all our walls
Like serpents to suck our spirits
Invisible yet overwhelming
Burdening the air with sorrow
Relentless in its humming
Pit-pat-pit-pat-pit-pat-pit-pat
Rapidly ferocious & murderous
Drowning those poor blooms
Left unattended on the terrace
In need of only a light spray
But clouds are always fickle
Unpredictable in their offerings
Sometimes an amorous drizzle
Or a knell for fateful endings

7. There are dried petals...

There are dried petals in a book
That I never did read
Pages slightly stained
From the long dead flower
Just like your declarations
of fidelity and reparation
for our near ruination
Your constant transgressions
The petals are a decade old
They smell like nothing now
Like the worth of your vow
When you handed those flowers
Hoping their scent would mask
The fetor of your foul lies
Oh how such simple tricks work
On vacuous love-struck eyes
I could still throw them out
These decaying reminders
Of a chapter that still stings
But I'll let them lay buried
In the book I'll never devour
Between blemished pages

For your memories don't hurt
At least not anymore
Maybe we can never keep
What the heart really needs
Maybe it's destined to bleed
For another loss we shall weep

8. The wind...

The wind betrayed me
It never sent any word
And then, the storm came
Like a capricious bird
Nesting while I was away
Waters sweeping the land
But I remained barren
A lone grain of desert sand

9. How are you...

"How are you?", my folks ask every day
So, I avoid most of their calls now
But I send them little notes of anguish
On every mode of messaging possible
Their daily 'good morning' texts are ignored
Or met with dispirited 'mornings suck', 'hate my job'
'Boss is a monster', 'Why work? I'd like to rob'
'Worked 14 hours yesterday. I think I am dead'
Who has the bloody seconds to think of 'how am I?'
But these little notes of anguish are gasps of fresh air
Until I can afford a therapist and get in their hair
My folks will pay my rent, not a shrink for me to vent
I send them enough stinkers almost every day
Yet they cannot see their kid's a little 'cray cray'
So little notes of anguish in their inboxes it is
'Drafted my resignation letter' is the best of it
Dads like us overworked, moms like us married
I'd like to dissolve, or die soon and be buried
Some move to goals & dreams, I have a death wish
Find me a genie or a witch to do a little 'swish swish'
If Santa existed or any kind of God of fortune
I would send them littles notes of anguish too

"Life has no point", "My mental health is in ruin"
"I have been a bad person, send death soon"
And when death comes to my door eventually
I would have a little note ready for it too
"You took too long, why so painfully slow?"
Hoping for good humour… an end to my show

10. Why is sorry...

Why is sorry such a small word?
Inept to make up for my callousness
When I made you cry for the first time
As you held a cigarette to your lips
Like its smoke would dull your pain
As I sat just a few feet from you
Unrepentant, gazing at those eyes
Reddened by slow silent tears
Your visage even more mesmeric
Stirring up waves of yearning
To clasp you in my arms again
To maybe never let go after all
But I was reminded of the distance
Miles that would divide us again
Like we were in parallel worlds
Each carrying on in our corners
Almost like the other didn't exist
My alarms at PM, yours early AM
We would have to steal moments
To hear the other over short calls
Surrounded by cold empty walls
It seemed a bye was always close

Like snapping it all was inescapable
So I called you, only to leave you
And a paltry 'sorry' will have to suffice
For the months we became strangers
For the days we never spoke
A 'sorry' is all I have got to say
But you came back to me anyway
Reminding me of what it was like
To not have those miles between us
To just exist in the same space
Would make cold winters warm
For it was January when you flew to me
A lost starling looking to rebuild its nest
And this time I wouldn't let go
But I am sorry about that summer
Such a measly word for an apology
Allow my embraces to help erase
The memories of a separation
There can never be enough of you
Even if we are cloistered the whole year
For I am no longer the same person
Who could imagine novel possibilities?
Or a life devoid of my January starling
Nothing could be complete anymore
Not for me, not without you
I am your nest, your home-shore

11. The floor...

The floor still has imprints of your feet
Fading each day, never from memory
There you have a permanent seat
Some days there are new moments
Dreamed up during fevered nights
Long walks; short thrusts; new flights
Kisses that never existed at all
Caresses that should've been there
Created when I needed them most
Comforting in snatches of sleep
In that fabricated corner, we never weep
For we are young and without flaws
Head's equal to a filmmaker at production
We are the lead actors, caked to perfection
A romantic tale with the cliched forever after
Playing each dawn, a tape of my favourite chapter

12. Why...

Why does it amuse you?
That I feel no need
For the touch of skin
That's not mine at all
Let intimacy be alien
If it needs tangibility
It won't find home or stability
Not in any part of my body
A bird's song is enough
The rain's fragrance is enough
Some book's story is enough
My own words are enough
To soften all hurt and blows
To forget all kinds of woes
This world tends to cause
To those who don't conform
To concocted standards of relations
As if some deity wrote a codex
A sacrosanct guide to love and sex
Warning deviants of hell's creations
Burn those books if they really do exist
For no God has the damn time to write

Only humans obsess over wrong & right
Forging fabricated stories rife with deceit
There's nothing to be amused about
If I seek not favours of the carnal kind
Because my wit is almost dried out
In thirst for a match of my mind
A person who can swap tales of wonder
Appreciate good poetry & clever prose
Curious, unafraid to make a blunder
Not a constant clown, nor always morose
Someone mirroring my inner grizzly bear
Who couldn't care less of what to wear
Who'd rather be with a tree, than another
We'd be independent, yet love each other

13. It's easy...

It's easy to wish ill-will
To hope you would lose
So it wouldn't be so hard
Accepting what you'd choose
A wild dream far from here
With too much sweat & toil
While I choose familiarity
The warmth of home soil
But I've loved you enough
To let go of petty desires
So I won't start fresh fires
And I won't fight you more
It's easy to wish ill-will
To hope you would fall
So I won't feel any regret
And break into a bawl
I've decided the hard way
To delete all your traces
Be it physical or digital
It's all now in backspaces
Let there be one last goodbye
No more of each other ever

It will be terrifying at first
Wistful memories at worst

14. I want to be...

I want to be as vague as a poem
With no longing to be understood
All you have to do is hear me out
Without interruptions, without doubt
Sure you might have questions
And feel like raising your hand
Save them for the last, dear listener
We have all the time for a rejoinder
Let's go back to the start now shall we?
I want to be as ambiguous as a poem
With no longing to be understood
Derive whatever meaning, it's all good
If I say I want to be a biscuit for life
It could mean being a sweet treat with tea
Or a trifling nuisance to feed the dog or a pet
Or the only dessert a poor person can get
If I say I want to be the deep blue sea
It could mean being endless and eternal
Or home to endless beings and their fate
Or a big pool for all of humanity to urinate
There can be countless tales to each little line
Hidden thoughts to every phrase I utter

Some jibes or jests to make hearts flutter
Interpret them however you would want
For I want to be as ambiguous as a poem
With no longing to be understood
Don't double-check with me, don't over-brood
I'll only say 'hmm', because to me... it's all good

15. We are like...

We are like two little plant pots
Hanging by an abandoned window
Fortunate to have those exact spots
The sun touching us with its glow
Old pipes dribbling nourishment
Rains reaching through as feasts
No doors to let in bereavement
Or even starving insects and beasts
A few feet apart, we keep thriving
Rare spells of drought barely daunting
Shrivel, shrink, fight & grow again
Soak the sun & share our pain
Had I been a lone forgotten sapling
Languishing by that rusted grill
Solitary survival wouldn't be a thrill
Death would be welcome to take its fill
You my friend have been the fence
Where my vines found strength to lean
Orphaned as we were, left unseen
Duality made grass our side green

16. If I had...

If I had words for it
There would be 100 books
A hundred-thousand words each
To get you within my reach
Stories from the tongue-tied
Hoping it would spell-bind
Not just heart but mind
That never look this way
Each book a huge leap
Their pages portals to you
If only it were that easy
But they are only phantoms
And can never really exist
For I have no pen or ink
And worse – no words
To write or even think

17. Our anxieties...

Our anxieties are invisible
like a stabbing in the gut
Unlike the ooze of a cut
On the skin of our lies
You've been breathing
And we've been fine
We've been waiting
For no word, no sign
If we cannot find home
in the stillness of our voice
It's pointless to roam
In search for some light
Even birds abandon nests
After they learn to fly
Fledging too soon… fatal
We could fall, we could die

18. I don't seek...

I don't seek art to gratify
To make what's wilted bloom
To be a beacon in a dark room
For it's not a magic broom
At least not for me to fly
Away from a broken nest
Somewhere else to rest
Bliss isn't as easily wrest
So I seek not art to gratify
But only for mild solace
And to just briefly erase
Thin tarns on the face
It's like floating dandelions
Small, elegant, mesmerizing
Like tiny clouds slow-dancing
Holding your gaze, distracting
For those few fleeting minutes
The self… coupling with a cloud
Weightless, in the air, unbowed
Without care, without roots

19. I don't need...

I don't need ears, or even eyes
For you don't ever talk to me
Yet you caress my skin
as if I were dear kin
You weep for my blisters
those dastardly brown spots
That've been ravaging my face
You wonder if it's just a phase
I don't need ears, or even eyes
To know all your sorrows
And how deeply you try
To stay sane, to not cry
For I've become your friend
Always where you last left me
Something you'll never lose
Even if I am no lover or muse
I don't need ears, or even eyes
To understand you do care
For my spots have been healing
And the stalks are finally flowering
They've brought out more smiles
Than one could hope to see on you

For I can feel it like the bright shining sun
When you caress my leaves one by one

20. How desperate...

How desperate have the times become
That we want to live on planets unseen
As if human nature dissolves in space
And will evolve into some unusual race
We are so broken that we will not fix
catastrophes of our own making
We'd rather find a new fairyland
Corrupt it up with the same old hand
Auteurs have envisioned distorted futures
Where kids hunt for potential homesteads
As adults perish battling lethal creatures
Perhaps hostility only hostility breeds
Very few fathomed the pandemic that spread
Fewer thought of global cities under lockdowns
In almost every corner death raised its head
Making trained doctors shudder in their gowns
Like every disaster ever, it too shall pass
But someday all of humanity could be grass
We could be extinct, the earth still alive
Without our chaos, it would only thrive

21. We don't always...

We don't always know what holds us captive
A bird in a cage may seem pitiful to some
But what if the bird is content right there?
With no desire to chirp free in the air
You might even open their prison door
But they won't flap their wings even a bit
Maybe even nuzzle against a metal bar
Dream of things within reach, not far
Guaranteed meals aren't luxury enough
Never in mortal danger, not relief enough
They may feel loved, they may never cry
For they don't know, what it's like in the sky

22. A song...

A song would be a simpler choice
To tell you sorry, to fix our rift
But I don't have that kind of voice
That inflects to sound like a gift
If I were to stand in front of a crowd
And break into your favourite classic
Not a single ear would be proud
Not even bad enough to be comic
So I am settling for a long-ish letter
But in the style of poets of the past
Poems make remorse sound better
And their charm seems to forever last
Remember when we were younger...
How we'd moon over the latest hit
Croon & shake to every damn banger
Like 'cool kids' who didn't give a shit
When did we lose those versions?
They disappeared without a trace
Like land lost to invisible incursions
We're different, yet the same face
I am sorry for missing milestones
The wedding, the first store unveiling

And that time you broke your bones
Sorry for assuming and never asking
Three stores, two dogs, a fine spouse
Perfect from an outsider's view
The cracks were inside the house
Your new walls, the ones I outgrew
Things should have never come to this
Each too far, drowning in a blue funk
Creating an abyss I didn't even notice
One couldn't rescue the other, if one sunk
So while you're still flapping to survive
Let me take that first step, to mend things
I'll be there for all your divorce hearings
Best-friends or not, to new beginnings...

23. I've cut someone...

I've cut someone maybe once in my life
One bloody time and we are all branded
As if we are out for murder, like a knife
Do they have to be so heavy-handed?
Those who give out names to things
Like numbered uniforms for crooks
Reducing them to nameless beings
Or maybe it's not as bad as it looks
For in numbers, aliases slowly fade
No reputation really left to wreck
But terrible sobriquets can ruin trade
Like a palm-sized blister on the neck
Of those who gratify to be paid
Some don't mind, don't crave fame
They're happy lying idle in the glade
But I don't take kindly to the name
It's an affront to be called a blade
Why make us pay for a few tiny nips
Barely any blood, or a scar to show
We are just leaves, not coarse whips
Don't call me blade, like a cruel foe

24. The little rushbird...

The little rushbird sat perched
Against blazing orange petals
Unlikely sight amid blaring metals
And the deathly sound of sirens
I never noticed the tree in bloom
Eyes always glued to digital screens
More adjusted to cosmetic scenes
Practically a virtual being in denial
Then one day an old friend knocked
We sat by a window, taking in the view
That's when I saw the flame of the forest
Or some prefer the crude 'bastard beak'
It stood among strangers, majestic in all its glory
The rare tree with more flowers than leaves
Also known as 'Palash', offered to Goddesses
Its beauty does befit otherworldly witnesses
'Love at first sight' must feel like this
Where a solitary being can fill you with bliss
Lightening your body, every muscle at ease
Tired eyes experiencing a rare sense of peace

25. To you...

To you, my dear friend
I've heard you haven't been in the best frame
Words are lightnings when one gains fame
Maybe you don't want to hear from an old pal
For what can I say that hasn't been said already?
To you the 'fading author', or so say the papers
Guess literary stardom lasts as long as vapours
Sorry, it wasn't my intention to stuff snark in
Let me remind you of something we read together
Perhaps a famous writer, a name is hard to recall
But their words were vivid like dried leaves in fall
They said don't worry if a story has been said before
For it might have been, but not by you
Not in your words, nor in your voice, not yet
There are millions, for who - you are the net
Your words the safety mesh they can fall on
X or Y or Z may say the same damn thing
But they don't have your flair, or your spark
Their voice has no light to reach in the dark
For some rooms can only open to your key
Don't abandon your readers, for they haven't you
Your books are lined up on our shelves with pride

Let critics do their job, it's not the time to hide
Sit up again in your beloved writing spot and speak
Write of your anguish if there's nothing else to say
A cut hurts the same, there's no originality to blood
It doesn't mean you cannot cry until there's a flood
Write what you must, and we are here to read

26. What would you...

What would you tell your younger self?
What's even the point of such questions?
To pick on ourselves for regrets and mistakes
Maybe pass them on to the younger snakes
For they bite you, on the back or feet
Crippling you when your bones ache most
And there won't be a neat cheat-sheet
Waiting to be delivered from future you
To alleviate the wounds you've gathered
Growing moss on your wits while rolling
Ignoring signs that were loudly glaring
Red flags, flashing over stuff that mattered

27. Dysmorphia...

Dysmorphia... what a strange little term
I see my body from a stranger's eye
Middling, vapid, a forgettable worm
Never metamorphosing into a butterfly
But I've suffered too long from this vision
A twisted sense of self, coated in derision
Of not being a painting, or even a muse
Yet it is all just an insecure mind's ruse
Takes too long to break self-made bastilles
Intangible shackles asphyxiate our doors
Senses cut off from beautiful blue shores
Everything worth doing in strangers' stills
It's not like we need photos for proof
The best memories exist only in our heads
But some of us have none under our roof
Each chapter in a day ends in prison beds
The body feels like a burden, a boulder
Dragging on in a daze as if pulled by a rope
Why doesn't it snap, why does it hope?
Drag... drag... drag... I keep getting older

28. They said...

They said I had faltered
That I was wrong to leave
That I had no right to grieve
The death of what was us
That I had no right to choose
The self over a broken fate
That it was better to wait
And hope for eternal spring
Our leaves were already brown
But everyone wore green specs
Blind to the winter flecks
And dead flowers on the ground
Some said it could bloom again
A little water & some more days
And it would grow in new ways
In different colours and shapes
But who knows what's to come
What if it's a pretty hemlock plant?
Lethal and final even during spring
Irreversible end a kiss would bring

29. Ants...

Ants... ants taught me the meaning of life
Also its futility, it's absurd pointlessness
A sugar cube's their deity, their royal highness
Oh how they work for it! entire colony on site
Spite the British, the Mongols and the Russians
Their empires pale against how ants have thrived
Colonies everywhere you'll find of these tiny ruffians
Save Antarctic, where even I wouldn't have survived
We see them often enough, strutting on kitchen floors
Moving like little cars driving away from food jars
All in a single line, like humans at shopping stores
Continually collecting, foraging, then heading home
Despite all my admiration, I've killed one too many
Wiping them out accidentally, without a glance
Their industrious little bodies rarely stand a chance
But each time it throws me into fleeting remorse
I wonder what they think of us bumbling giants?
We are no deities, fairies or monsters to fight
Just fools they steal from, occasionally bite
Their day too packed to give us any mind
Ants have more purpose than great philosophers
Their seconds not wasted in drafting frilly witticisms

Never holding back over anticipated criticisms
Yet all their grit turns to dust with a quick little swat

30. I've only felt...

I've only felt my forehead today
heavy, in constant knots
rest of the body disappearing
like none of it mattered
only the head exists
with fears & unfounded anxiety
with hatred in all its notoriety
a thinking being no more
when such rage takes over
words laced with hurt
bruising all those around
the mind first relishes it all
then bleeds most from the fall

31. Myths...

Myths from the past are a wonder to the ear
Like the one with Zeus condemning entire humankind
Splitting our form into two, to forever the other find
A body of four limbs, two heads, separated in his fear
What kind of a God is scared of humans seizing power?
To tear us apart, so we keep looking for the other half
Does this inflicted agony make the thunder God laugh?
If it weren't for love, could we make the Gods cower?
What of those who've lost all faith in Eros & its arrows?
Or the lucky few who find their parts sooner than later
Do they prepare for war after their fill of inflamed nights?
Or simply get consumed in flesh, food & domestic fights...

32. The air...

The air feels lighter
Quilt softer, heavier
Its warmth addictive
Sleep's lure seductive
Just one day away
From dreadful Monday
This morning I can lie
Forever on my bedside
Limbs don't even try
Don't move, they hide
From the dizzying light
Holding covers tight

33. Some days...

Some days are out of a bad movie
The direction chaotic, muddled
One could belt tracks that are groovy
Won't drown mundane beats of life
So you dread the approaching end
confused over what to expect
every little turn a terribly drawn bend
but unpredictable in all its shades
Who knew dispirited events could hold surprises
Nothing exciting about a new gash
Or the unfamiliar pain that rises
Through your chest or the throat
The med cabinet overflowing now
thick with remedies of all kinds
all sorts of illnesses can take a bow
once a pop of color finds its way
All the way from my throat to the pit
slowly washing away the day's pain
from sick bones come something fit
fresh from a fight on the insides
But every day won't see resolution
things will only get worse, and worse

from new woes will come a new solution
but until then you live in the dark
Like in a badly produced indie short
where nobody knows how things end
Ball not even in the maker's court
For all they say is – 'go with the flow'

34. Blue...

Blue, like the water I drowned in
Black, like the colour that kicked in
Olive, your skin against the sunlight
Grey for a second, for I gave up the fight
Olive again, you were back in sight
More color, as I prepared a goodbye
Blue again, the eyes could see the sky
Me in your arms, saved.. how? why?
And then you said the first 'hi'.

35. Who knows...

Who knows what visage smiles behind screens
Doctor, singer, philosopher, poet, or engineer
We can get a coating of our desired veneer
Embellishing details, like famous movie scenes
Some days 20 sounds a good number, other days 40
A struggling model, a widower, or a bored student
Sometimes just a mysterious prick playing hard to get
Always a simple moniker, something easy to forget
'Dawn', 'Purple Haze', 'Lost Cause', 'Day Tripper'
Songs make fine titles for an online drifter
Surprising how nobody asks, 'what does it mean?'
'Age, sex, location' is all anybody wants to glean
You meet all sorts of folks, with all sorts of tricks
Animals in digital heat hitting click click click
It's all repetitive, like deja-vu on bloody loop
Yet addictive, like alcohol, without it you droop
I recently met a therapist, or so they claim
Who spun stories that'd put Kings to shame
Got a number & an address, so wish me luck
First session soon, might be worth the buck

36. Show me...

Show me your Gods, not in your books or statues
Ask them to walk on our roads or our plateaus
Where do they live? Where do they sleep?
If they are awake forever, do they blink? Do they weep?
Ask them why their wrath's reserved for human beings
Ask if they appreciate the symphonies your choir sings
Do they have the time to listen to individual prayers?
Or the millions might as well prostate for their mayors?
Ask why non-believers haven't been burnt to dust
While children are mutilated, sold for a kidney or a lung
Why innocents are torn apart by material lust
The 'good' called early, why some sinners die young?
A writer struck gold writing a story of the millennia
Perhaps a ruler or a tribal lord seeking order & favour
The original bestseller, fantasy-fiction before paper
Flying chariots, magical beings, folks walking on water
Maybe your God is nothing but Superman of a lost era
Created by an oppressed soul seeking redemption
Or an imposter playing God to oppress the gullible
One blind sheep is enough for a flock's destruction
Until you can show your Gods, not in books or statues
In tangible form, walking our roads or plateaus

It's easier to believe they were nothing but tricksters
Maybe royals, priests, magicians, good old fraudsters

37. They can...

They can ask us to shut up
They can send murder threats
They can wish for our downfall
Put a date to it, even place bets
They can call us ugly, unwanted
They can label us 'bile' or 'trash'
They can make memes & posters
Get creative, sell them for cash
They can run smear campaigns
They can attack us from all sides
Nothing remains the same for long
Not even the mightiest of tides
Victory comes to the last one standing
They can brand us whatever they want
They will get tired, eventually move on
We will continue, exactly as we want

38. Maybe...

Maybe I have exhausted all emotions in a turbulent past
So don't call me unfeeling or someone who will cry last
Not if you haven't lived my life, or cohabited for a while
Not if we haven't even exchanged so much as a smile
Broken birds that cannot fly, continue to have feathers
But external signs can't always measure one's worth
Don't draw judgment from rumours spread by others
Draw courage instead to ask me questions upfront
Nobody can promise conclusive answers, nor shall I
Patience was never my virtue, so don't expect details
Maybe I'll just pass some of your queries, don't ask why
Maybe I am one of those magical foxes with many tails
Shapeshifting at will, having lived hundreds of lives
Back filled with crimson scars from a thousand knives
Cynical with experience spread over dozens of decades
Tired of excessive drama, of eloquent human charades
So don't claim there are pebbles in place of my heart
A hundred times over I may have played your part
And yes, I have exhausted all emotions in the past
It's damn well fine if I never cry or finish last

39. Broken...

Broken are the roads to our hallowed home
We fall into incalculable cracks to never recover
Wallowing in self-pity, rejecting external aid
Weeping profusely for foiled plans, once well laid
Home isn't always bricks or stones or logs of wood
Sometimes it's just conjured up visions of the future
Slowly disappearing from our tightly clenched fists
Subjugated are we... by invisible cuffs around wrists
Perhaps there exists an apathetic gene
That makes one slow, feckless & mean
Never one to act, but sharp with wisecracks
Stuck in the same spot, belittling passers-by
Such is the fate of an incompetent dour fox
Calling grapes sour, devouring rot for a living
For some who fall in muddied holes are rescued
Then there are others who make it their dwelling

40. Pull...

Pull out your favourite writers
Sing in new tunes beloved quotes
Let their words water your boats
To coasts with everything aplenty
Too many have achieved too much
Merely on borrowed words or thought
So sponge away... maybe not get caught
If a net does ensnare, bite with might
Denounce detractors, swear by your soul
Claim some God whispered in your ear
Divine parlance poured crystal clear
Written in your holy book turned gold
I always find it hard to memorise lines
poems, proverbs, lessons from the wise
everything hard to repeat, even easy lies
Who knows… these could be stolen sighs!

41. There's a familiar...

There's a familiar stranger inside me
instructed to keep its voice down
Yet it screams through town
Making me the street oddity
The cuckoo talking to nobody
Yet, I'd be lying if I said it's terrible
The unhinged seconds desirable
Satisfaction surpassing embarrassment
You'd know if you held debates within
Letting arguments slip out sporadically
In unintentional bursts, often manically
Making bystanders frown in derision
So I try to keep those voices down
Only while out and about in town
But my stranger is charmingly witty
So oftentimes I remain street oddity

42. People...

People in my life have changed over time
But I am still singing the same old songs
Maybe art outlives our passing whims
Staying eternal, its glow never dims
Why do we not tire of familiar tunes?
But grow out of childhood bonds pretty soon
Could be distance, or something else, who knows
No common ground or glue to hold us close
Yet, our favorite songs are always with us
Imprinted in our memories like love itself
Thousand times over, lyrics eager to be heard
Years on mute, yet you never forget a word
Perhaps it's that soothing stillness to music
Its ability to freeze moments attached to melodies
Like the first time we danced through night lights
Or a road-trip materializing after spirited fights
A jazz piece or a pop rage cannot inflict wounds
Maybe open some, yet offer comfort like none
Easing anxieties, healing harrowing wrongs
And so I am still singing the same old songs

More Titles By Sneha Jaiswal

Bad Town Kids

A coming-of-age tale of four small town kids who lose a friend to an untimely death.

Love, Loss, Lockdown

A quirky collection of 10 short stories loosely set against the Covid19 pandemic.

Death & Darker Realms

A collection of 40 poems exploring various themes.

Connect With The Author

INSTAGRAM

@Writer_Jaiswal

TWITTER

@Writer_Jaiswal

FACEBOOK

@WriterSnehaJaiswal

Printed by Libri Plureos GmbH in Hamburg,
Germany